Inspirational Insights

Updated Edition

RESILIENCE IN THE FACE OF CHALLENGES

DR. CLARICE FLUITT

ISBN: 978-1-7331216-0-6

Publisher: Clarice Fluitt Enterprises, LLC
P O Box 15111
Monroe, LA 71207
www.claricefluitt.com
www.claricefluitt.org

For Worldwide Distribution

Dedication

To My Lord and Savior, the Giver of Life, the Imparter of Wisdom, and the Master Teacher

Acknowledgments

It is with profound thanksgiving that I acknowledge the endeavors, input, insight, and wisdom of my literary companions, Executive Assistant Dr. Tandie Mazule and Administrative Assistant Dr. Evon Peet. Their persistent persuasion and fortitude combined with the heart and vision for this project have proven that they both aspire and strive toward something higher than oneself and impart the very breath of life that awakens, completes, and fulfills its purpose. They have become two of my "keys of life" that are interwoven with the "test of time" to produce a consortium of invaluable and timeless *Inspirational Insights*.

My Interior Designer, Carol Martinez, has become one of our own and brings dimension, character, and personality to every written page. My book would be incomplete without her expertise and unwavering resolve to expand the horizons that produce the marks which distinguish this work from all others. For that, I am deeply indebted.

Endorsement

Inspirational Insights are powerful keys that will challenge your thinking and cause you to go higher as you walk them out. The experience of new levels of success in every area of your life is often encumbered by fallacious facts that are not truth, and truth that is not believed and activated. We are all people making choices but should never take a journey through life without a map and some guidance. Dr. Fluitt presents some incredibly valuable yet practical insights that few others ever think through. We can easily become our own worst enemy when we find ourselves unknowingly agreeing with negativity. Through the practice of making Inspirational Insights a part of our daily routine, thoughts can ultimately become transformed into patterns that can refresh, re-fire, refine, and restore us back to the knowledge of the truth of our fabulous, fixed, and ultimate purpose.

KATIE SOUZA
PRESIDENT OF EXPECTED END AND
KATIE SOUZA MINISTRIES, AND PUBLISHED AUTHOR

Table of Contents

Foreword

This is a wonderful book full of precious jewels of wisdom. It is much too rich to breeze through in a single sitting. Imagine, if like a sponge you could absorb the keys to life's happiness, success, fulfillment, love, honor, and peace. Imagine, if once those keys became firmly planted as truth in your heart they began to bloom with divine knowledge and understanding to direct you into your life's destiny. What would your life look like then? My experience reading this book of insights gleaned from a life of worship and intimate relationship with the Lord Jesus Christ has shifted my POVOL (point of view of life).

The foundation you choose to stand upon determines your outlook and sets your expectation. If you are on the fence watching life pass you by, this book will help you get off that "critical observer" perch and enter the fray as an active participant in pursuit of your dreams. It will help you change your mind, which will change your destiny, and serve as your compass to fulfillment. Simply put,

Clarice Fluitt is a gifted phenomenon; a woman who has spent her life mining the deep mysteries and treasured wisdom of the very purpose of life itself and the means to achieve its ultimate prize. Every pair of eyes that will perceive and pursue these precious insights will prosper, improve, fulfill, and enrich their life in the realms of time and all eternity. I love this book. I love this wonderful woman of God.

SHIRLEY SEGER
CEO / CO-FOUNDER
XPMEDIA.COM, INC.

LIFE LESSONS

A Teachable Moment
Dr. Clarice learning from her mom at age 4

Why Should We Awaken Our Dream?

While watching the local news, there was a most inspiring and motivational report of why we should have a dream.

In the small town of Natchitoches, Louisiana, a woman was recognized for her prolific book writing skills. She was all smiles as the T.V. reporter conducted a personal interview with Ms. Dixie Dee. Ms. Dixie was 101 years young. With very limited funds, friends, and family her dream was to save enough money so that, when her time came to go, she could have a proper burial.

She had a large Maxwell House coffee can that she put her money in for her big day. After over 30 years, Ms. Dixie had plenty of money for her going away party! Then, she heard that there was something called a www. com and her original dream was re-fired. She took all her burial money and, at the age of 89, bought her first computer and started writing and publishing her own books!

Mr. Scrambled Brain, as she affectionately referred to her computer, helped her achieve her lifelong goal of becoming a writer. At 101 years of age, Ms. Dixie Dee has penned and printed seven books, and continues to write. She has never been afraid of old age, says any ego is a key to achieving your dreams, and informs all that you are never too old to learn a new trick!

Ms. Dixie Dee on her computer

It is never too early or too late to believe and achieve your dream!

... for with God all things are possible.
Mark 10:27

Don't Lose Your Keys

I was impressed by the words of the famous football coach, Mr. Vince Lombardi. He said, "Leaders aren't born, they are made," just like everything else, through hard work. This is the price to pay to achieve your goals in life.

I encourage the earnest reader who is desiring a positive change for their life to use these "keys to success" to open all the effectual doors set before them. These doors can lead to the fulfillment of those God-inspired dreams, visions, prosperity, and legacy.

Those who never activate the "keys to success" should know that it is only due to their lack of discipline, structure, and focus. They are those who desire the benefits of success but choose not to embrace the procedure to change.

Remember, not to decide is a decision. Please don't lose your keys!

Things Are Not Always as They Appear

My husband George is a very kind and generous man who is blessed with a 100% choleric personality. This means that once he has decided on something, he is so completely convinced of his opinion there is no further need for discussion. His core motivation is to overcome all opposition to his thoughts or plans. So, if you ever talk to him, be sure you have your facts straight!

Here is an AH HA moment in the lives of George and Clarice. I asked George to buy some cherries at the grocery store. He smiled and said he would. When he returned home, he commented on how fresh and plump the cherries were. I was unpacking the groceries and looked at the box. They were not cherries at all. They were cherry tomatoes!

I said, "Honey, these are not cherries. They are tomatoes." Without even looking at the box, he said, "Dear, read the label on the box. It says cherries." There was such an absolute knowing in his tone. He was so convincing that I had to look again at the box and then pick one of the cherry tomatoes up to taste it. I said, "George, these are tomatoes; not cherries." He picked up one of the "cherry tomatoes" and jokingly said, "I knew that all the time. I was just checking to see if you were paying attention."

We both had a good laugh. He said, "Isn't this what you teach others about being engaged and attentive? If you are going to talk the talk, you must walk the walk."

Now, I am convinced he did not know he had mistakenly bought the tomatoes because, at the time, he was not focused and his mind was wandering. Details were not remembered and the facts were not important. But that is just my opinion after being his wife for over 50 years.

Falling for the Crowd

This is a true story about a very gifted motivational speaker. She was excited and waiting to go on stage to speak at the nation's No. 1 Business Seminar. One of the most influential motivational speakers in the world was introducing her. He was extolling her gifts and abilities and personally endorsing her politely; and NOW, Ms. Wonderful!! The atmosphere was electric.

The crowd gave a rousing welcoming applause. The confident speaker stepped on to the stage and immediately tripped and fell face-forward onto the floor! The audience gasped, he was shocked, and the lady had a millisecond to decide to be a victim or a victor. She was helped to her feet and, while her mind was trying to convince her that her hands, knees, and chin were not broken, she immediately summoned her inner strength and got up!

She knew he was deeply concerned and visibly shaken as were all the staff and crew backstage. The lady approached the shocked audience, took a deep breath, paused, smiled, and said, "I know you guys are going to love me because I fell for you from the start!"

A thunderous applause sent the message from the audience that they all saw the fall but, they all also saw her get up! She immediately had favor with the crowd. Her message was not only audible but visual, and she presented an unforgettable presentation of how to be an overcomer.

Don't waste your sorrows. Get up!

> *For though the righteous fall seven times, they rise again . . . Proverbs 24:16*

WORDS OF WISDOM

Knowledge of a Truth Does Not Mean You Have an Experience!

Although you may be aware of a certain truth, although you may have learned or gained information, only knowledge that has been combined with an experience will give you the completed sum total of that which constitutes the whole. Allow me the opportunity to assist you in transforming your parts and pieces, your ideas, your incompletes into a unified and desired plan that accomplishes your innermost goals and desires.

A Person with an Experience Is More Valuable than a Person Who only Has an Opinion!

To have had an experience is to have been in direct participation or observation of an event or activity; the conscious events that make up an individual life. When we come to understand that our opinions, our views, our judgments are merely appraisals formed in our minds without us having lived through, undergone, or encountered something personally, we then discover that our opinion is open to dispute. Embrace the process of exchanging that which is open to dispute with that which is practical and applicable to your life's plan and purpose.

Your Opinion and How You Think about Failure Can Determine How High You Will Ascend As You Climb the Ladder of Success

As we discover that opinions are open to dispute, and that failure is generally thought of as falling short in some area or being deficient in some way, a total and complete reversal of our thoughts about failure can transform the attributes of failure into character, integrity, and excellence. Your thoughts about failure can be reversed to create an atmosphere that is filled with success and distinction.

Reflecting on Your Past Failure and Pains Will Not Bring You into the Now!

It is interesting that reflection is described as bending or folding back, similar to an image in a mirror. While we desire in our innermost being to soar to new and greater heights, its accomplishment is quite certain to result in static interference when our mind is consumed with what used to be, rather than what could be. My heart is to position people for the successful present, the today, the currently, this moment in time.

Life Draws Life

You will draw to yourself what you are releasing in the atmosphere with your countenance, conduct, and conversation. As a magnet possesses an extraordinary power or ability to attract because of its characteristics, so also do you have the extraordinary power to unleash through your expression, management, and discourse that which you choose to draw to yourself.

Find People that Celebrate You

Internalizing your failure kills the seedbed of dreams and visions. Surround yourself with positive people, positive conversations, and positive attitudes. Find people that celebrate you, not just tolerate you. They are those who see your potential, affirm your presence, admire your ambitions, and approve your path. The positive people in your life will assist you in the process of taking your dreams and visions to the place of accomplishment, achievement, and performance.

CELEBRATE YOU!

All Opportunities Come with:

A. Doubt: the lack of confidence

B. Unbelief: skepticism

C. Discouragement: to lose heart

D. Analysis paralysis: powerless and endless examination

E. Excuses: alibis and the absence of ownership

With each promotion, each advancement, each breakthrough comes your opportunity to be the creator of your atmosphere that converts potential into reality.

How to Embrace Change and Be Resilient in the Face of a Challenge:

A. **Refuse to be offended;** strike insult and outrage from your every thought.

B. **Respond, but do not react.** Keep opposition at bay and leave revenge alone.

C. **Do not let anyone see you sweat.** Stay flexible and recover quickly.

Shocks are meant to be withstood with no permanently damaging effects.

Champions live differently than ordinary people.

When Priorities Compete with Each Other:

A. Priorities cannot compete with each other until they are first established.

B. Stay true to yourself and always let integrity go first.

C. Always take the high road.

Utilize the Power of Proximity

As you surround yourself with those who celebrate you and your life, attain to greater heights through the process of intentional connections. Those of influence who are close to you, acquainted with you, and have something you desire are those who can be of great benefit to your promotion and advancement. A broader understanding of this principle is sure to assist you up the ladder of success toward your ultimate aim in life.

Learn to Listen and Practice being Fully Engaged

Open more than your ears; open your entire being to what is said, including the between-the-lines dialogue. As you journey through this process, you will soon accomplish independently the discipline of hearing with intention.

Be Prepared when Opportunity Presents Itself

There is nothing worse than the curtain going up, coming down, and leaving you standing in the wings. Make yourself valuable to others, not obnoxious. It is interesting that value is described as something expensive, extravagant, precious, and premium while obnoxious is not only unpleasant but also harmful.

Outsource by Surrounding Yourself with Smart People

It is often the easiest and most productive way to accomplish the most in the least amount of time. What you might not be strong in, someone else is. What they might need help with, you can in all likelihood provide. Rather than trying to be the hero and the end-all to all things, learn how to leave the sweat behind and run the course with less difficulty and interference.

Negotiate to Win

It has been a long-standing motto of mine to make your deal going in rather than trying to evaluate the loss factor after it has become impossible to recover. A win-win situation is without dispute, can often be handled and managed successfully before compromise turns into conflict, and is beneficial to all parties involved. You stand to gain everything without losing anything.

Always be True, Fair, and Genuinely Interested in Others' Success

The degree or measure that we enjoy our own success is directly proportionate to how true, fair, and interested we are in the success of others. Examine the differences between interest and envy, that which is favorable to both sides, and genuine authenticity versus imitation.

Thawing Your Visions and Dreams

Honor your commitment to yourself. The reason most people fail is that, when you decide to do something and you do not do it, you diminish your sense of self. You have to face the man or the woman in the mirror when you do not follow through with your original commitment to your dreams and visions.

RELATIONSHIPS

Dr. Clarice at age 6 with her mom

Discretion

"Discretion is the better part of valor."

William Shakespeare

"Discretion is the better part of valor" means that it is regularly good to think very attentively before doing something that you will regret later in the future. Caution helps avoid future problems.

He that walks with wise men shall be wise, but he who keeps a companion of fools shall be destroyed. Stay with wise people, those who fear the Lord. When you and I are standing as ambassadors of Christ, our countenance, conduct, conversation, and the way we honor one another reflect that redemption in the face of all people.

There is nothing more detestable or frustrating than arrogance. There is nothing more limiting for a person than arrogant dishonor. Boosting your own ego by relating information that is personal only to you, dropping names that benefit only you, and giving out personal information that belongs only to others is a sure path toward future regret.

Give and Take

Honor is an amazing thing. It becomes like an airborne virus when you begin to activate it in your own life. Honor begins with you; the honor you have for yourself. You see, until you can love and honor yourself, you really cannot love or honor anybody else. By modeling honor and respecting others with your countenance, conduct and conversation, people see how to treat others, and how to be treated.

Sensitivity and Truth

We often find ourselves surrounded by people that may not hold to the values we hold to as far as our faith is concerned. Honor is the willingness in your heart to reward someone even though they are different. There is the sound of honor that comes from us as we speak kind words to others. Honor can be taught. It is not an anointing. It is not a gift. It is a decision that transcends culture and condition.

Reciprocity

Those who honor you qualify for a different relationship than those who dishonor you. Those who sow into your life with goodness should not be taken for granted. Those who do kind things for you and believe in you should expect reciprocity. It is much more than just a part of life. Someone honoring you is a gift from God. Wherever you find people who honor you, reciprocate with kindness, and return the honor by sowing it back to them.

"While I know myself as a creation of God, I am also obligated to realize and remember that everyone else and everything else are also God's creation." - Maya Angelou

Honor

Learning how to order our conversation to be righteous should be among our top priorities in life. It is not how smart you are or how talented you are; it is how much love is in you to honor others. Honor carries within it a sound, a resonance and a vibration, a frequency of like things that begin to speak to each other. Those good things God has imparted to us will suddenly go deep inside of others as we speak to them in honor.

What is the Seed for Access?

Honor is the seed for access into any environment, in any season. Honor those who are in authority; child to parent, student to teacher, employee to employer, citizen to political position. It does not matter that you do not fully understand them. They are different from you specific to their position of authority. You do not have to agree, but you do have to honor. What and who you honor will come back to you.

HONOR

SECRETS TO BUILDING FRIENDSHIPS

Be Authentic

Be yourself and others will respond with equal authenticity. This is the secret to building friendships. Be genuine and choose to spend time with those that respond in like manner.

I have developed a time-proven skill on how to be authentic, attentive and sensitive with those that I meet. It is simple; just be nice, smile, and express a sincere interest in others.

I travel extensively and have the opportunity to connect with a diverse group of people. I have learned that people know when you genuinely care about them.

I was in the Dallas airport on one occasion and saw a group of weary soldiers. Their destination was Afghanistan. I was moved with compassion as I approached these young men and women and said, "Hey guys, thank you for your service to our country!" Suddenly, their smiles acknowledged their appreciation of my attention toward them. I assumed an authentic motherly tone and asked their permission to pray for God's protection over all of them. They quickly stood up, removed their hats, and bowed their heads as I prayed. We all hugged and expressed love for one another. While this may not have been politically correct, it was not only scripturally based but carried with it the expression and essence of the kind of authenticity that will last a lifetime.

Dear friends, let us love one another, for love comes from God. Everyone who loves has been born of God and knows God. Whoever does not love does not know God, because God is love. – 1 John 4:7-8

MAKING HARD
DECISIONS

Without a Decision There Will Not Be a Change

You can count on having the opportunity to make some hard decisions concerning your family, finance, friends and your faith.

I want to share some positive thoughts on making hard decisions without feeling condemned or fearful. When we have to confront a difficult situation, we should have a plan before we decide to take action. The Bible tells us there is no haste in Zion and your mom probably told you, "to slow down, haste makes waste." A decision will not necessarily produce a change in our challenges. But, without a decision there will not be a change. Here are some helpful insights for when you are confronted with a hard choice:

A -**Ask God for wisdom**; the ability to use knowledge skillfully and to make the right choice (Proverbs 16:20-21).

B - **Back up,** take a realistic picture of the situation, and get clarity so you can see the benefits and consequences of your choice (Luke 14:31).

C - **Calculate;** ask yourself what is the worst that could happen?

Prepare yourself with all the information and resources available to you so you can make your deal going into your challenge. Do your homework, forgive everyone, and keep your faith strong in the Lord (Mark 11:24-25).

D - **Don't doubt yourself.** Be courageous and stand up for truth, integrity and all that you truly believe in. For God has not given us the spirit of fear; but of power, and of love, and of a sound mind (2 Timothy 1:7).

E - **Enumerate your benefits;** all decisions positive or negative will have far reaching effects. Believe for a win; win for all involved. Trust God for His purpose (Romans 8:28).

F - **Feel good about yourself.** When you have done all you can do, then all you can do has been done. Avoid the temptation toward "analysis paralysis" over your decision.

G - **Gather wise advisors.** Do not make life changing decisions in a vacuum.

May these thoughts be added to your arsenal of acquired wisdom and help equip you in your decision and choices. Together we have the mind of Christ.

Living the Good Life

Life Is More than a Destination

Let me encourage you with some things I have learned about living the good life. It is logical to my mind that life is indeed a gift from God. Life is like a journey; it can be fulfilling, or it can be difficult and unsatisfying.

Life is more than a destination from point "A" to point "Z." It was not given to us to simply eat, sleep, reproduce, and die. Life is an amazing developing process consisting of strategies, habits, rules, starts and finishes. God's ladder of success is always inviting and challenging us to climb higher into the ascended life. Many situations that we consider to be walls that separate us from our dreams and goals are not walls at all; they are God's call that demands great leaps of faith on our journey.

Priorities

"The purpose of life is a life of purpose."
~ Robert Byrne

In my journey I have learned many things about true happiness and success. A person can accomplish amazing things and create massive fortunes without ever experiencing true purpose or happiness. I have learned a real secret for success. A person's priorities must be in alignment with our Creator's blueprints or goals for our lives. Confidence in yourself is necessary. Confidence in your Creator is essential.

Passion and Purpose

Much of our success in life is a result of our own choices and behaviors. The decisions we make on our journey will be both positive and negative. The poor choices we make should not include playing the "blame game." Neither should we consider hosting a "pity party" when we fall. For though the righteous fall seven times, they rise again, but the wicked stumble when calamity strikes. So get up!

We must have passion and purpose to respond to life's challenges. We alone are responsible for our own happiness. Take responsibility for your life.

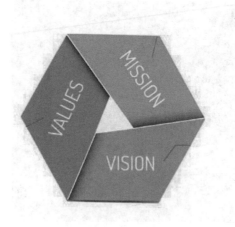

ASK DR. CLARICE

What Is Heaven like and what Is Hell like?

Heaven is traditionally thought of as the location and dwelling place of God and His angels and saints.

Hell, according to the Christian view, is a place or a state in which the souls of the damned suffer the consequences of their sin eternally. Hell can be defined as the eternal fate of the unrepentant sinner who used his free will to choose not to choose God.

Theology 101: Here is a very simple definition.

Heaven
Heaven is good.
God is good.
Eternity is really good.

Hell
Hell is bad.
Devil is bad.
Eternity is really bad.
Choose one.

For God so loved the world, that he gave his only begotten Son, that whosoever believeth in him should not perish, but have everlasting life.

John 3:16

Do you have a balanced diet?

We have many restaurants in our town that are cafeterias. Their specialties are to serve a diversity of food choices. Customers can select from a large variety of healthy foods. They have the meats, vegetables, salads, treats, breads, etc. all displayed. When the immature are not supervised in choosing their food, we can witness some very poor and unbalanced meals being chosen, consumed, and wasted.

I have discovered that some immature Christians eat from the Word of God in like manner. They love the prosperity and healing bar and cannot get enough of the sweet stuff. They will neglect taking a large serving of patience, stewardship, or any long suffering. Selah.

We can get fat on too much sweet stuff and lose the motivation to serve the cause of Christ.

Choose to eat the whole Lamb, not just the lamb chops. Eat the feet of the Lamb and embrace His walk. Eat the inward parts of the Lamb and grow the heart of love and compassion. Eat the tongue of the Lamb and develop an appetite for edifying and not complaining.

The next day John saw Jesus coming toward him, and said, "Behold! The Lamb of God who takes away the sin of the world!" (John 1:29)

Oh, taste and see that the Lord is good;
Blessed is the man who trusts in Him!

Psalm 34:8

Why shouldn't we be anxious about the future and how can we have peace?

We are being bombarded daily with disturbing news as the perversity of media madness exposes every ungodly activity imaginable. I should also mention immoral movies, heathen television, gangster music, violent games, etc., etc. They are wicked, demoralizing, and deceptive.

The Word of God instructs us that the time will come when mankind will call good evil and evil good. Well, it's here!

I cannot allow the clouds of destructive wars, rumors of war, and all the evil reports of despair and injustice to blind my faith and love. I am seeing the Word clearly; the Kingdom of God is an unshakable Kingdom. While everything else is shaking, don't move. Stand steady and release God's Word of life. You can create goodness with the fruit of your lips. Do not give up your dominion! Though the battle rages, the war is won!

Do not be anxious about anything, but in every situation, by prayer and petition, with thanksgiving, present your requests to God. And the peace of God, which transcends all understanding, will guard your hearts and your minds in Christ Jesus.

Philippians 4:6-7

How do you know the difference between God's voice and the voice of another?

When I was a child, my father would gently say, "Honey, it's time to go to bed. Put your toys away, brush your teeth and I'll be in to hear your prayers."

My response was, "In just a minute." I continued doing whatever it was that I was interested in at the moment. Then the voice of my father came with a simple sound that was measurable, audible, and timely. It was a sound without any confusion or unbelief on my part. It contained direction and application. He said, "Clarice, NOW!"

I immediately knew I had heard authority and I desired to comply with my father's words. His voice was undeniable. He was my father, and I was his child.

When he has brought out all his own, he goes on ahead of them, and his sheep follow him because they know his voice.

John 10:4

Is it enough to just believe Jesus is the Son of God?

What does believing in Jesus require?

Does the Devil believe in Jesus?

Acts 16:31 instructs you to believe on the Lord Jesus Christ and you will be saved, you and your household. This wonderful promise does not guarantee that all our loved ones are saved because we are. Each must believe for themselves with an action faith, not a dead profession.

> *You believe that there is one God. Good! Even the demons believe that—and shudder. – James 2:19*

James does not set faith against works, but discusses two kinds of faith; a dead faith and a saving faith. Saving faith is not simply a profession or an empty claim, nor is it merely the belief or acceptance of a creed. Saving faith will produce an obedient life to Christ.

The word believe is a verb and demands action. A believer is a noun; the name of a person, place, or thing. It denotes identity.

The demons believe. This is an adjective meaning and describing mental ascent, not a saving faith. They tremble and are struck with fear.

Saving faith is alive and active. Dead faith is hopeless.

What has your experience taught you to avoid?

My experience has been that walking with God is a no whine zone.

> So all the congregation lifted up their voices and cried, and the people wept that night. And all the children of Israel complained against Moses and Aaron, and the whole congregation said to them, "If only we had died in the land of Egypt! Or if only we had died in this wilderness! Why has the Lord brought us to this land to fall by the sword, that our wives and children should become victims? Would it not be better for us to return to Egypt?" – Numbers 14:1-3

In this text, the Israelites murmured against their gracious and loving God and God did not like it.

To murmur means to grumble, whine, or complain.

Some contemporary words related to a whiner are as follows: complainer, cry baby, loser, annoying, wimp, brat, jerk, fault finder.

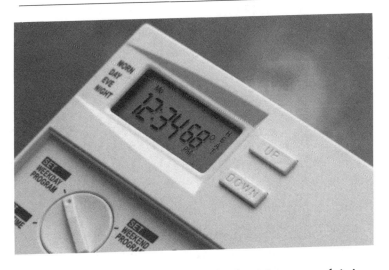

I have learned not to anger God with a complaining negative attitude. The Scripture says the steps of the righteous are ordered by God (Psalm 37:23). Now beloved, if you believe that is true, then every time you complain you are finding fault with God and His plans.

You can live your life as a spiritual thermometer and always report on how hot or cold things are, or you can become a spiritual thermostat and change your atmosphere from too hot or too cold to just right.

Avoid whiners and find winners!

What is the first thing you plan to ask God and why?

These are my thoughts on the what's and why's to ask God when I see Him face to face. I think I have talked enough so I plan to spend eternity listening and agreeing with God and beholding His glory.

> *But we all, with open face beholding as in a glass the glory of the Lord, are changed into the same image from glory to glory, even as by the Spirit of the Lord. - 2 Corinthians 3:18.*

INSPIRATIONS

Don't Give Up

Scriptures:

So shall My word be that goes forth from My mouth; It shall not return to Me void, But it shall accomplish what I please, And it shall prosper in the thing for which I sent it.

— Isaiah 55:11

You have seen well, for I am ready to perform My word. — Jeremiah 1:12

Devotional:

Webster says a miracle is an event or action that contradicts known laws; a remarkable event of nature; hence, a supernatural event.

In 1992, I was in Boulder, Colorado, to attend my daughter's wedding. My husband and I were riding to the service with my daughter's future father-in-law who is a federal Judge of Jewish descent, and his lovely wife.

As we were driving, the Judge was relating to us his encounter during World War II when his company came under a terrible siege. After sharing this event with us, he said, "That was the luckiest day of my life! Artillery fire hit and killed several of my buddies in that foxhole. I was the lucky one. I lived."

As he continued to drive, I touched his shoulder and simply said, "Sir, maybe it wasn't luck at all. What if it was God's love for you, and that part of the plan He has for your life was to provide for your protection." He made no response and we quietly proceeded to the service.

Although the Judge has since gone home to be with the Lord, at the age of 92 while still living, I received an amazing call from my son-in-law telling me that the Judge wanted to speak to me about receiving Jesus Christ as his Messiah! My husband and I booked our flight and left immediately for Cincinnati.

After our arrival, we met with the Judge who lovingly took my hands in his and with tears in his eyes said, "Do you remember the time we were in the car and I was telling you about my escape from death during World War II, and do you remember what you said to me?" I responded with a "yes." He said, "Your words have pierced my heart all these years. I cannot escape the thought that God loves me and I am ready to believe and receive Christ as my Messiah."

It has been a few months since we prayed with the Judge. His continuing confession of faith in Christ is very powerful.

It took 21 years for that seed of conversion to grow. God has an appropriate time for all things so do not ever give up on your prayers. Continue to decree, declare, and proclaim the Word of God. It will not come back void but will accomplish what it is sent to do as He watches over His Word to perform it!

Beyond the Natural

Scriptures:
And let us not grow weary while doing good, for in due season we shall reap if we do not lose heart. - Galatians 6:9

Behold, He who keeps Israel shall neither slumber nor sleep. - Psalm 121:4

Devotional:
We are admonished in Galatians 6:9 not to be weary in well doing. Isaiah 40:31 declares that they who wait upon the Lord shall renew their strength; they shall mount up with wings like eagles, they shall run and not be weary, they shall walk and not faint.

There is an antidote to hunger, insomnia, and weariness.

When the disciples asked Jesus about eating, He said, "I have food to eat you know not of." I recall the story of how an angel gave food to a prophet and he outran horses for over one hundred miles.

A generation will arise that will activate the realm of the miraculous with the faith of God! I am excited to hear of those who have decided to agree with God and believe that with God all things are possible. His divine intervention produced babies in old and barren Sarah, Hannah, and Elizabeth, and restores the youth of those who satisfy their mouths with God's Word.

There are so many miracles and promises of God just waiting for His people to go beyond their tradition and comfort zone. Consider this: The law of gravity is a reality but so is the law of lift. For a hundred thousand tons of airplane to rise and fly, the law of lift must employ the law of gravity. One does not negate the natural to embrace the supernatural.

All things are possible to those who believe. The kinds of manifestations demonstrated in the lives of those who are daring to believe God's Word could be carrying the answer to world hunger, weariness, insomnia, and fear in all forms. Psalm 121:4 tells us that God Himself neither naps nor slumbers.

The Kingdom of God is within the redeemed. We are taught to declare that the Kingdom of God has come in me. It is also Biblical truth that God's habitation is in the believer. We are learning how to let God arise, and unbelief be scattered. The days ahead are promising for glory to be revealed.

Now is the time to stop and shout!

Union and Communion

Scriptures:

That I may know Him, and the power of His resurrection, and the fellowship of His sufferings, becoming conformed unto His death.

– Philippians 3:10

Devotional:

Philippians 3:10 is the deepest cry of my heart. I believe I am called to help instruct those who have been awakened to bridal affections for King Jesus.

I am a spiritual "bridal consultant." In the natural, a bridal consultant's responsibilities include instructing and overseeing the essential preparation for a wedding. They must know the proper protocol, acceptable etiquette, the proper dress, and how to conduct a wedding rehearsal.

As a spiritual bridal consultant, I always recommend to those who desire union and communion with Jesus to read the Song of Solomon. Here you will find the pattern for true love and mature spiritual growth.

The transforming power of the Holy Spirit is realized through the Song of Solomon, and its compelling love language invites believers to abandon themselves to a life of full surrender to Christ and become the companions of like nature and ability that must rule now and throughout all of eternity.

I hear the Lord's compelling invitation for intimacy, "Come into Me and you will see."

Find the Right Fit

I have come to the conclusion that the phrase "one size fits all" is a complete misnomer. I can walk into a store with my friend and try on a "one size fits all" poncho. I can hardly get it over my head. My friend tries on the same one-size-fits-all poncho and, on her, it looks like a circus tent that 4 other people could fit into. One size does not always fit all. One solution is not always practical for every person in every situation. One idea that works for one sounds like complete nonsense to another. While it is in the realm of wisdom that we should all be surrounded with those who give us sound insight and input, we must also remember that we are created as unique individuals endowed with creativity and our own distinct uniqueness from the ultimate Creator.

What are your thoughts about one size fits all?

Sensory Overload

Ask anyone who knows me and they will tell you that I love a multitude and variety of colors, textures, sounds, and images; all in the same place at the same time! There is, however, something to be said for being quiet in color, texture, sound, and image; it's called focus. Although I might draw energy from an atmosphere and environment filled with sensory stimuli, I have learned over the years that concentration follows quiet where my attention is directed toward one thing instead of my mind being spread abroad in several directions. I have also learned that it takes discipline, and an intentional deliberate choice to sit in a room devoid of sound, left with only my own creative ideas which, when given half a chance, I am always amazed by!

What steps do you take to quiet yourself?

Relevance

I had an opportunity to change everything I knew about how to communicate with others. When an opportunity comes that takes you where you've never gone before, you will sometimes find yourself in need of learning a new language. At the age of 72, I found myself embarking on a whole new career that required me to learn a whole new language. I realized that, in order to be relevant, I needed to be able to communicate in a way that my new audience would not just understand, but would be able to relate to and apply to their personal and professional lives.

I have learned during my journey down the road of a new career that, had I not been willing to embrace change, I would end up trying to make old stale moldy food look pleasing to the eye and be tasty to the palette of a new, fresh, and exciting generation. Do not underestimate the importance of being relevant to those that cross your path. You never know what the power of a relevant message can accomplish.

Have you ever had to revise the presentation of your message to align with the impact you desire on a whole new audience?

Bridges

Bridges come in all shapes and sizes but their purpose is the same; to link one thing to another. It's interesting that this connection has to be made on both sides. A bridge connected to point A but disconnected from point B serves no purpose. Even a draw bridge that separates in the middle has to be connected at both ends to fulfill its purpose. A bridge in its most typical display spans rivers, canyons, mountains. But a bridge in another expression spans a life from one season to another. It's called transition. Like every other bridge, on the landscape of our lives the connection between point A and point B remains in place. However, the significance of realizing we have reached our seasonal destination rests in the opportunity to look back across the bridge of our lives for the purpose of seeing how far we have come from where we started.

What does your bridge look like?

The 'Athlete' Principle

Athletes learn early on what attention to the task at hand is all about. One of the first things they learn about themselves is their personal style of focus; what takes their head to the practice, preparation, and game, and what keeps it there. Research shows that some athletes perform best when they focus their attention on internal cues, while others perform best when focusing on external triggers. Either way, the main point is that, because they know their focus style, the next step becomes so much easier; disciplining their minds and managing their focus in such a way that distractions take a back seat to performance.

What steps do you take to get and maintain your focus?

Resilience

I love to watch little toddlers that are just learning to walk. They finally get to their feet, let go of whatever they might have been hanging on to, take a few wobbly steps, and fall down or sit down rather abruptly. Then they get up and off they go again, only to fall down. Each time there is a fall, the distance between this fall and the last increases until finally their falls become very infrequent and their walks turn into runs. Children are some of our greatest teachers when it comes to having the ability to bounce back quickly. They somehow seem to instinctively know that the quicker they rebound, the quicker their goal can be realized. It does us well to remember these little ones and that, what comes instinctively to them, requires of us when we fall an intentional and disciplined act on our part of pulling ourselves up by our bootstraps, dusting ourselves off, and moving on.

Turning Signals

What a wonderful invention. It's nice to so easily be able to let people know when you are considering changing direction. At the click of a lever or push of a button everyone around you is made aware that something is changing. It prepares them to know how they must adjust their positioning to accommodate your change in direction. Have you ever been following behind someone in a car who decides at the last minute to change lanes, or make a sudden right or left turn? How easy it would have been to signal their intention. Instead, their impulsive undisciplined reckless action put everyone around them in danger. As with life in general, it behooves us to stay aware of the signs that signal a change in direction intentions, and eliminate subjecting those we live or work with from getting blind-sided by your decision.

Conclusion

The Power of Accountability

Everyone needs someone who will lovingly critique them; a sparring partner to keep them in top shape and who is not a yes ma'am or sir person. Find someone who knows, loves, and appreciates you. Allow and accept the valuable input of another set of eyes and ears. Let me assist you through the process of ownership, accountability, and accepting responsibility for your decisions and show you how that process invariably leads to living at a standard of excellence not attainable if you are an island unto yourself.

My favorite book says that without a vision the people will die, and without a progressive vision they will grow lazy and careless. Do not settle in yesterday's success but instead gather your strength to leave a legacy that says, "You gave all you had while you were alive."

It is this philosophy I desire to impart to those I coach, those I love, and those I journey through life with. It is this process I can assist you with if you will allow me into your life and the progressive successes of your "now."

Inspirational Insights

About Dr. Clarice Fluitt

Dr. Clarice Fluitt is a powerful international speaker and industry leader. She is a highly sought after personal advisor, author, and life strategist whose message brings inspiration and innovation to every audience she encounters. Dr. Fluitt's insight and delivery have solidified her position as a renowned motivational speaker and transformational voice impacting countless lives daily.

As a global trainer for more than four decades, Dr. Fluitt's success is based on her ability to help organizations thrive for real results. Her experiences as corporate and executive coach, entrepreneur and strategic consultant allow Dr. Fluitt to share her proven strategies for building customer value, creating revolutionary products, inspiring innovation, and generating sustainable growth. She takes the time to understand your organization and your audience, and delivers an informative and highly engaging presentation that will help you and your teams achieve results.

Dr. Fluitt has shared the stage with some of the world's most influential pioneers in the industry to include Steve Forbes, Suze Orman, Larry King, Michael J. Fox, Rudy Giuliani, Les Brown, Daymond John, Rick Belluzzo, Shaquille O'Neal, Joe Montana and many other legendary speakers. Dr. Fluitt's direct approach to transformation is crafted and customized to ensure that every audience is equipped with the tools they need to succeed in today's economy.

More Resources by Dr. Clarice Fluitt

Books
Ridiculous Miracles
The Law of Honor
Thoughts that Make You Think
Living the Unhindered Life
Developing Your Limitless Potential
Think Like a Champion and Win
Experiencing the Power of God's Word
Re-Script Your Future

For information on Real Results Solutions Coaching
and Mentoring packages:
Visit: www.realresults.solutions

Contact Information
Clarice Fluitt Enterprises, LLC
P O Box 15111
Monroe, LA 71207
Phone: 318.410.9788
E-mail: drclarice@claricefluitt.com

Websites:
www.realresults.solutions

www.claricefluitt.com